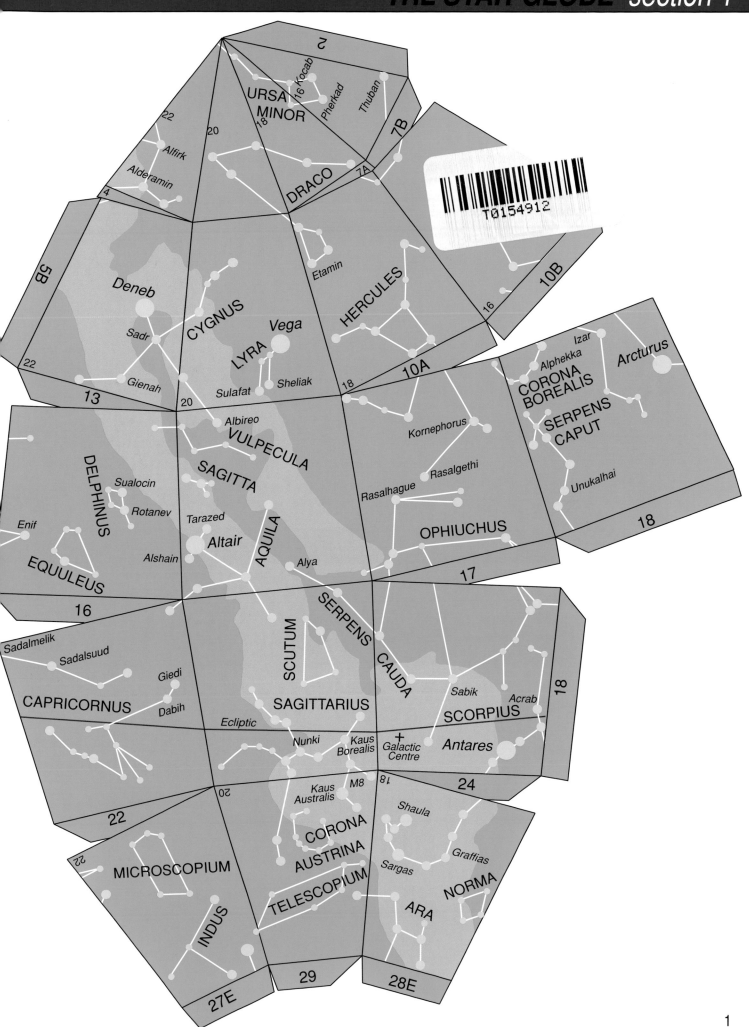

T0154912

1

7B

7B

7A

4

10B

10B

10A

13

13

17

16

16

24

22

24

22

2

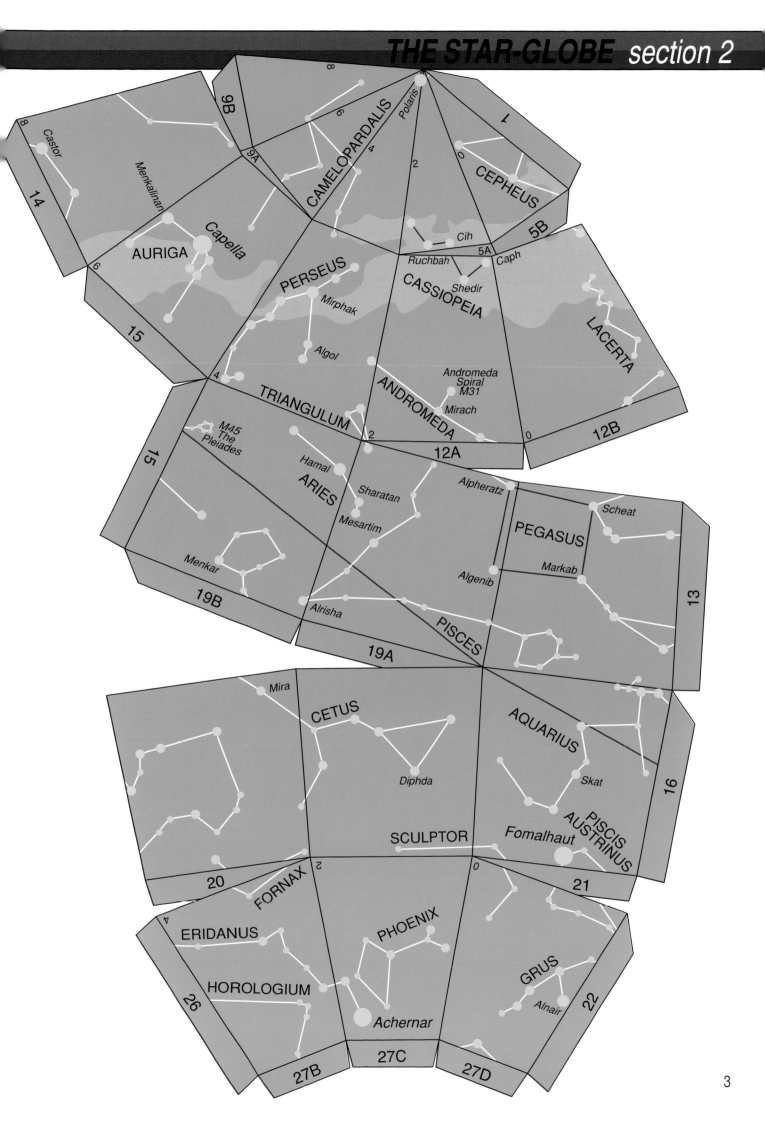

3

9B

9B

9A

5B

5A

5B

12A

12B

19A

19B

19B

21

20

8

2

11B

6

11A

17B

17A

17B

25

18

25

23A

18

23B

1. Remove the six pages which make the minibook.
2. Score along the lines marked ◄————►
3. Cut out precisely.
4. Fold away from you to make a hill fold.
5. Assemble the five sections to make the 20 page minibook.

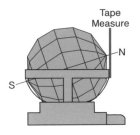

Do a careful check that the pages are in the correct order.

6. Fix them together. If you have a suitable stapler, then that is probably the easiest way. Otherwise use a needle and thread like the bookbinders of old!
7. Store the minibook in the stand drawer.

The TARQUIN Star-Globe

BACKGROUND INFORMATION
Experiments, facts and ideas about the celestial sphere.

Cut out the Quick Card while looking at this side and then keep it in the drawer to remind you how to set up the Star-Globe.

OBSERVING THE SKY IN THE NORTHERN HEMISPHERE

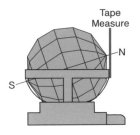

Tape Measure

N

S

The axis of the Star-Globe must always be in a north-south direction with the north celestial pole at an angle of latitude above the northern horizon.

1. Set the calculator to the date and time. Remember that it shows the local time and so if 'Summer Time' is in operation, deduct one hour from the clock time.
2. Read off the R.A. number from the outer edge and then turn the Star-Globe so that the meridian with that number leads between the north celestial pole and the northern horizon.
3. Use the tape-measure to check the angle is still the angle of latitude.
4. The sky is then set up for the correct date, time and latitude.

A more detailed explanation is given in the minibook.

STELLAR MAGNITUDES

The brighter a star appears to be, the larger the size of the dot which represents it.

Magnitude 1   Magnitude 2   Magnitudes 3, 4, 5   Magnitude 6

The stars printed on the Star-Globe include the brightest 51 stars of magnitudes 1 and 2 and sufficient others to clearly mark the constellations.

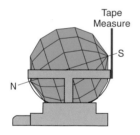

The dates given on this chart are the ones when the Sun is officially in each of the twelve constellations of the zodiac. Because of the precession of the poles, the real Sun is at the present time about one sign further on than shown by the official dates. Indeed the Sun now passes through a thirteenth constellation, Ophiuchus being the extra one. You can see this by following the ecliptic around the Star-Globe.

Score and fold, then cut out looking at this side.

When you have assembled the minibook and no longer need to use the instructions overleaf, cut this section out, keeping well away from the outlines. Then fold along the score line and glue back to back. Then cut out precisely and store the card in the drawer.

THE QUICK CARD

OBSERVING THE SKY IN THE SOUTHERN HEMISPHERE

Tape Measure

S

N

The axis of the Star-Globe must always be in a north-south direction with the south celestial pole at an angle of latitude above the southern horizon.

1. Set the calculator to the date and time. Remember that it shows the local time and so if 'Summer Time' is in operation, deduct one hour from the clock time.

2. Read off the R.A. number from the outer edge and then turn the Star-Globe so that the meridian with that number leads between the south celestial pole and the southern horizon.

3. Use the tape-measure to check the angle is still the angle of latitude.

4. The sky is then set up for the correct date, time and latitude.

A more detailed explanation is given in the minibook.

STELLAR MAGNITUDES

The brighter a star appears to be, the larger the size of the dot which represents it.

| Magnitude 1 | Magnitude 2 | Magnitudes 3, 4, 5 | Magnitude 6 |

The stars printed on the Star-Globe include the brightest 51 stars of magnitudes 1 and 2 and sufficient others to clearly mark the constellations.

The TARQUIN
Star-Globe

BACKGROUND INFORMATION
Experiments, facts and ideas
about the celestial sphere.

Tarquin

0 906212 60 X

Tarquin Publications, 99 Hatfield Road, St Albans, AL1 4EG.

THE CELESTIAL SPHERE

An astronaut floating in space can turn his head and body and look out in all directions. It is as if he is at the centre of a huge sphere with all the stars marked on it. It is called the CELESTIAL SPHERE. The Star-Globe is a three-dimensional model of what he could see. The pinpoints of light which we call stars are in fact like the Sun, but enormously far away. Although they are all printed on the same Star-Globe, that does not mean that they are all the same distance from us. Not at all. The celestial sphere is just a convenient way of representing their relative positions in the sky, seen from a point in space in the neighbourhood of the Earth.

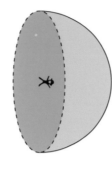

Of course our imaginary astronaut could only stay in space for a few hours. Real astronomers and real people who are interested in the stars and planets live on the Earth and cannot see out in all directions because the Earth itself gets in the way. In fact even on a flat plain, we can only see half of the celestial sphere at any one time. Also for exactly half of all the hours in the year, our half of the celestial sphere contains one exceedingly bright object, the Sun. So much light comes from the Sun that we are dazzled and all the other stars which make up the celestial sphere become invisible to us. The periods of time when the Sun is not in our half of the celestial sphere, we call 'night' and it is then that we can observe the stars and planets, weather permitting.

Because the Earth is rotating, the celestial sphere appears to rotate in the opposite direction and the portion of the sky we can see at any one time changes hour by hour. The part of the celestial sphere which is visible at any moment depends on the latitude, the date and the time. With the aid of the Star-Globe and the calculator you will be able to find out what the sky is like from any place on Earth, on any date and at any time. To do this, you must understand how it represents the night sky and then how to set it correctly in its cradle.

1

STAR QUIZ

If you think that you have mastered the use of the Star-Globe, then these questions will test you and also suggest some other ideas and investigations.

1. In Paris (48°N), when is Orion highest in the sky at 8.00p.m. local time?

2. In which year will Jupiter join the heavenly twins Castor and Pollux?

3. When during 2012 are Venus and Jupiter close together? Are they visible in the morning or the evening?

4. How far south do you have to be so that the Plough completely disappears below the horizon for a few hours each night? How far so that it can never be seen at all?

5. Is there anywhere on Earth where you could see all the stars in the celestial sphere at least some time during the year?

6. Notice that in Aswan in Egypt (23.5°N) the star Sirius always rises above the horizon on a bearing of about 110°. At what time of year does Sirius rise just after the Sun has set?

7. On February 24th 1987 at 9.00p.m., the supernova 1987A was seen for the first time by the amateur astronomer Albert Jones in Nelson, New Zealand (41°S). What was its bearing and elevation?

8. When does the Sun set exactly in the West and rise exactly in the East?

9. From Earth, the Sun and the Full Moon each subtend about half a degree. On the scale of the Star-Globe what diameter should the sticky circle representing them have? Consider size not brightness.

10. Find the time of sunrise and sunset at 72°N on July 1st.

If you have enjoyed making this Star-Globe, then there are other books which might interest you. In particular 'THE TARQUIN GLOBE', 'THE SUN, MOON & TIDES' and 'SUNDIALS & TIMEDIALS'. Tarquin books are available from Bookshops, Toy Shops, Art/Craft Shops, and in case of difficulty directly by post from the publishers.
For an up-to-date catalogue, please write to Tarquin Publications; 99 Hatfield Road, St Albans, AL1 4EG, England.
Alternatively, see us on the Internet at www.tarquin-books.demon.co.uk

INSIDE OR OUTSIDE?

The celestial sphere can be represented perfectly by a map printed on either the inside or the outside of a true sphere. However, if the chart of the stars is to be on the inside surface of a sphere, then the sphere must be large enough for people to get inside. This is exactly what happens when you visit a planetarium. You sit under a spherical dome and a special apparatus projects the stars and the planets onto the inside of the roof above. The projector moves and can be operated so that the movement of the stars during a whole night is portrayed in just a few minutes. The apparatus is also adjustable for different latitudes and seasons. In a show lasting about 30 minutes you are able to get a very good understanding of how the stars and planets change their positions during the course of the year.

For a Star-Globe, the chart of the stars is printed on the outside of the sphere in such a way that the stars remain in their same relative positions.

Star-Globe
looking from the outside.

Capella

Cassiopeia

Real Sky or Planetarium
looking from the inside.

Notice that Capella is to the left and lower than Cassiopeia in the real sky and it is to the left and lower on the Star-Globe. Also if you look round to the right on the Star-Globe, then that is equivalent to turning right when outside at night. The stars which are directly overhead in the real sky are at the top of the Star-Globe when it is correctly set up.

Once you have got used to looking at a Star-Globe, then it is equivalent to having a small planetarium of your own which can be adjusted and set however you wish. It shows where all the brightest stars are and gives the names of the constellations. The brighter a star appears to be, the larger the size of the dot which represents it. On page 13 there is an explanation about how the brightness of stars is classified, using MAGNITUDES.

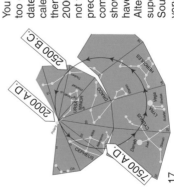

| Magnitude 1 | Magnitude 2 | Magnitudes 3, 4, 5 | Magnitude 6 |

The stars printed on the Star-Globe include the brightest 51 stars of magnitudes 1 and 2 and sufficient others to clearly mark the constellations.

2

THE STAR OF BETHLEHEM

Many people have wondered what the Star of Bethlehem could have been. Traditionally, the Wise Men came to Bethlehem by 'following a star' which 'stood over the stable where Christ was born'. Some people have suggested that it could have been a supernova, an exploding star, which shone brightly for a few days or weeks at the critical time. However, a supernova would not wheel across the sky during the night along with the other stars. It is also difficult to imagine how anyone could say that it 'stood above the stable', even if it passed directly overhead at Bethlehem. How do you follow a star which moves across the sky each night?

The Star-Globe enables you to test an interesting theory, because it can be set to the sky over Bethlehem which is at 31°N. Now Canopus is the second brightest star in the whole sky and it can just be seen from Bethlehem. Set the Star-Globe to latitude 31°N so that Canopus is due South. You will see that it is just above the southern horizon and as the Earth rotates, it quickly sets. From the vicinity of Bethlehem it can only be seen on a bearing which is virtually due South. Suppose the Wise Men were crossing the desert and were heading South. Every night they would see the bright star shining on the horizon in just the direction they wished to go. Could they not be said to be 'following a star' which 'stood over Bethlehem'? Using the calculator we can even test at what time of year the situation arises. When the Star-Globe is set correctly, the meridian between 18 and 19 leads between the north celestial pole and the northern horizon. If we set the dial to midnight and the 'answer' to between 18 and 19, the date can be seen to be December 25th. How remarkable.......but!.....

THE PRECESSION OF THE POLES

You may think that the argument given above is too good to be true, and it almost certainly is. The date of Christ's birth is not known exactly and the calendar has been adjusted by twelve days since then. Also the events described took place about 2000 years ago and the north celestial pole was not then close to Polaris. The Earth's axis precesses in a circle which takes 25,800 years to complete. A Star-Globe drawn then would have shown the whole sky shifted. Would Canopus have then been visible from Bethlehem? Alternatively, could there perhaps have been a supernova in just that portion of the sky far to the South? We shall probably never know, but it is very interesting to speculate.

17

11

THE STAR-GLOBE

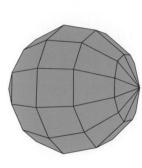

A true sphere cannot be made out of flat sheets of card and so the shape of the Tarquin Star-Globe has to be an approximation. However, it is a very convenient way of representing the celestial sphere, even if at first sight it appears to be a curious shape. It clearly shows the system of celestial coordinates which help us to find the positions of all the stars in the night sky.

Because the Earth is rotating, the celestial sphere appears to rotate in the opposite direction around the same axis. This axis, called the CELESTIAL AXIS passes through the north and south celestial poles, just as the Earth's axis passes through the north and south terrestrial poles. The time for one revolution of the celestial sphere is 23 hours 56 minutes 4.1 seconds. This is called a sidereal day (from the Latin 'sidus' - a star or a constellation). For convenience a sidereal day is also divided up into 24 equal 'hours', which are slightly shorter than normal hours shown on a watch. The difference is only about 0.27%.

THE CELESTIAL AXIS

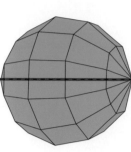

The positions of the stars on the celestial sphere are represented by a system of latitude and longitude, like that used for places on the surface of the Earth. However, they are not called latitude and longitude, but DECLINATION and RIGHT ASCENSION.

The celestial equator divides the celestial sphere into two equal halves, just as the real equator divides the Earth into the northern and southern hemispheres.

DECLINATION - CELESTIAL LATITUDE

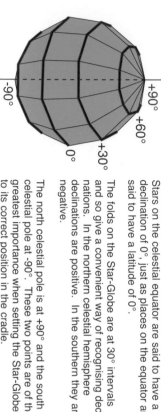

Stars on the celestial equator are said to have a declination of 0°, just as places on the equator are said to have a latitude of 0°.

The folds on the Star-Globe are at 30° intervals and so give a convenient way of recognising declinations. In the northern celestial hemisphere declinations are positive. In the southern they are negative.

The north celestial pole is at +90° and the south celestial pole at -90°. These two points are of the greatest importance when setting the Star-Globe to its correct position in the cradle.

THE MILKY WAY

The Sun and all the individual stars that we can see in the night sky belong to our own galaxy, which appears to be quite a typical one. It is in the shape of a flattish disc with spiral arms, but we cannot see it like that because we are inside it. If the galaxy is indeed flattish, we could expect to see a greater density of stars when looking along its plane rather than looking elsewhere. This is confirmed by the existence of the MILKY WAY. On the Star-Globe it forms a band of lighter colour and it shows where the density of stars is much greater. The lighter band passes right round the celestial sphere and a section through it gives us the direction of the galactic plane.

THE GALACTIC CENTRE

When we look towards the centre of the galaxy, we know that we are looking at the greatest density of stars. The sky does not, however, seem brighter in that direction because so many of them are obscured by great clouds of dust. It is thought that there may be a black hole close to the centre of the galaxy, but of course we cannot see it. No-one can see a black hole, no matter how powerful the telescope, because the force of gravity is so great that not even light can escape from it. It is an amusing thought that the dust may be obscuring something that we could never see directly. It is a bit like wearing a blindfold in the dark!

SUPERNOVA

Sometimes a star explodes giving out an enormous burst of energy. Suddenly a bright new star appears in the sky. Such events are very rare and the last observed one in our galaxy was in 1604. Since the first telescope was invented in 1609 there has not been one to observe. However in February 1987 a supernova was seen in the Large Magellanic Cloud. The L.M.C. is a galaxy-like collection of stars which is loosely associated with our galaxy. Although it is 170,000 light years away which means that the explosion took place 170,000 years ago, the supernova could be seen clearly with the naked eye from latitudes south of 20°N. It was called 1987A and is marked on the Star-Globe. Much scientific work was done and it has given many useful clues about the nature of matter and the life cycle of stars.

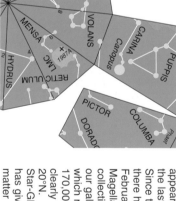

RIGHT ASCENSION (R.A.) - CELESTIAL LONGITUDE

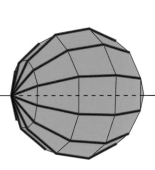

The celestial sphere has meridians which join the north and south celestial poles, just as the Earth has meridians of longitude which join the Earth's north and south poles.

Celestial longitude is not measured in degrees, but in hours of RIGHT ASCENSION. This is usually shortened to R.A. Because the celestial sphere completes one revolution in each sidereal day, each star must cross the Earth's meridian through the place of observation twice a day. It crosses once above the celestial pole and once below. It is the time for the lower transit which is called the Right Ascension.

On Earth the zero line of longitude is the meridian through Greenwich. On the celestial sphere the zero is chosen as the place where the apparent track of the Sun (THE ECLIPTIC) crosses the equator as the Sun passes from the southern to the northern hemisphere in Spring. This point is called 'THE FIRST POINT OF ARIES' or the 'VERNAL EQUINOX'. The exact time of the Vernal Equinox varies a little from year to year, but it is within a day or two of March 21st. The star Sirius has a R.A. of 6.45 hours and it crosses the meridian 6 hours and 45 minutes (of sidereal time) later than The First Point of Aries. The folds on the Star-Globe are at 2 hour intervals of R.A. and form a useful grid system when finding stars and constellations.

LOOKING AT THE NORTH CELESTIAL POLE

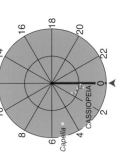

LOOKING NORTH

At the Vernal Equinox, the zero line of R.A. at midnight leads between the northern horizon and the north celestial pole.

LOOKING NORTH

At 4.30 a.m., four and a half hours later, the sky looks like this.

Since the Pole Star is very close to the north celestial pole, it is always due north of the observer. The grid system and all the other stars appear to rotate around it at a steady rate. These diagrams show the positions of Capella and Cassiopeia, which are always visible in the night sky at latitudes north of 50°N.

4

LOOKING BACK INTO THE PAST

Light travels at the enormous speed of 300,000 km/sec, but even so it takes time to travel through space. The light from the Moon takes 1.3 seconds to reach us and the light from the Sun takes 8 minutes 20 seconds. This means that if we look at the Moon or Sun we do not see them as they are now, but as they were some time ago. If the Sun were suddenly to disappear, we should not know about it until 8 minutes 20 seconds had elapsed. So great are the distances in space that light from even the nearest bright star system, Alpha Centauri, left on its journey 4.3 years ago. Perhaps when you look at Sirius you could try to think what you were doing 8.6 years ago, because that is when the light which is entering your eye left on its journey of 8,100,000,000,000km.

This table shows the time that light has been travelling before it reaches you. Whenever you check the direction of north by looking at Polaris, you are looking back into the middle ages.

Astronomers with sensitive instruments can look even further back in time and thus hope to understand the history of the universe. They can even trace some radiation, which is the residue of the Big Bang which took place more than 15 billion years ago.

Moon	1.3 seconds
Sun	8 mins 20 secs
Vega	27 years
Capella	42 years
Antares	250 years
Deneb	400 years
Rigel	500 years
Polaris	700 years
Andromeda Spiral	2,300,000 years

ISLANDS IN SPACE

Stars are not evenly distributed in space, but are grouped together in associations called galaxies. Galaxies come in many different forms, but predominately they are flattish and spiral shaped and each contains tens of billions of stars. The nearest spiral galaxy to ours is the Andromeda Spiral which can be seen with the naked eye in good conditions. Astronomers with powerful telescopes have been able to observe galaxies in all directions. There are billions of them within the range of modern telescopes.

Plan view

Side view

15

13

FINDING THE STARS

It is a good idea to look up some of the brightest stars on your Star-Globe. By doing this you will be able to practise using the system of Declination and R.A. and at the same time become familiar with the names. Since the names mostly come from Greek, Latin or Arabic some hints about pronunciation are also given.

NAME	PRONUNCIATION	R.A. h. m.	DEC Degrees
Aldebaran	al-deb'a-ran	4.36	+17
Altair	al-tair'	19.51	+ 9
Antares	an-tar'reez	16.29	-26
Arcturus	ark-tour-us	14.16	+19
Betelgeuse	bet'el-gers	5.55	+ 7
Canopus	ka-noe'pus	6.24	-53
Capella	ka-pell'a	5.17	+46
Deneb	den'eb	20.42	+45
Polaris	poe-lar'ris	2.32	+89
Procyon	pro-si-on	7.39	+ 5
Regulus	reg'-you-lus	10.08	+12
Rigel	rye'-gel	5.15	- 8
Sirius	si'-ree-us	6.45	-17
Spica	spy'ka	13.25	-11
Vega	vee'ga	18.37	+39

CONSTELLATIONS

The pattern of stars in the sky is so complicated that it is very difficult to remember them without help. The ancients, in particular the Greeks, grouped the stars into patterns which they thought resembled animals, birds, mythical people or creatures. For instance the pattern of stars in the constellation Leo were thought to resemble a lion.

It needs a very vivid imagination to see them like this but since some method of classification is needed, the old names have stuck and are still used today.

LEO THE LION

THE ZODIAC

The Zodiac is the name given to an imaginary band around the celestial sphere which includes the paths of the planets, the Moon and the Sun. It is centred on the ecliptic which is the path of the Sun and which passes through twelve constellations. These twelve equal parts of the celestial sphere are known as the SIGNS OF THE ZODIAC.

Name	Meaning	Official Dates
Aries	the Ram	Mar 21 - Apr 20
Taurus	the Bull	Apr 21 - May 21
Gemini	the Twins	May 22 - Jun 22
Cancer	the Crab	Jun 23 - July 23
Leo	the Lion	July 24 - Aug 23
Virgo	the Virgin	Aug 24 - Sept 23
Libra	the Balance	Sept 24 - Oct 23
Scorpio	the Scorpion	Oct 24 - Nov 22
Sagittarius	the Archer	Nov 23 - Dec 22
Capricorn	the Goat	Dec 23 - Jan 20
Aquarius	the Water Carrier	Jan 21 - Feb 19
Pisces	the Fishes	Feb 20 - Mar 20

THE PRECESSION OF THE EQUINOXES

When the idea of the zodiac was first developed in ancient Babylon, the Sun was actually in the given constellation on the official dates. If you compare the position of the Sun today using the calculator and the Star-Globe, you will find that it is about one sign out of step. This is because the Vernal Equinox, which is the zero of the meridian system, moves about one seventh of a degree westward each year. This may not seem much but it means that 'The First Point of Aries' is now in Pisces! In fact star charts like the Star-Globe have to be updated every 50 years or so to maintain their accuracy. The basic plan for the Star-Globe was based on Epoch 2000 which means that it will be good enough until the year 2025.

ASTROLOGY

This is the ancient art of foretelling the future from the positions of the stars, the planets, the Moon and the Sun. It probably started in ancient Babylon and ever since then Kings and Emperors often had an official astrologer at court whose job it was to warn about possible dangers which the stars foretold. The detailed study of the sky which this work entailed was a most important influence on the development of scientific astronomy. In fact, many of the earliest astronomers were primarily employed as astrologers. Gradually the development of scientific thought made it harder and harder to believe that the destiny of an individual could be influenced by changes in the position of planets millions of miles away. However, even today, all over the world newspapers and magazines print advice based on 'what the stars foretell'. Millions of people certainly enjoy reading about it and regard it as a harmless superstition. Others take it very seriously and will not take any important decision without reference to their horoscope or a reading of the stars by an experienced astrologer.

HOW BRIGHT ARE THE STARS AND PLANETS?

The faintest stars which can be seen with the naked eye in good conditions have a brightness roughly equal to a single candle seen from a distance of 10km. This amount of brightness, which is the threshold of vision is called one unit.

Using that scale, the star Sirius has a brightness of 1080 units. It is equivalent to 1080 candles at a distance of 10km. The next brightest is Canopus with 550 units. These two are quite outstanding and they are far brighter than any others. Around 200 units there are several, including Vega, Capella, Arcturus, Alpha Centauri, Procyon etc.

There are only about 20 stars in the whole sky which shine with a brightness of 100 units or more. There are about 200 which shine with a brightness of between 100 and 10, and a further 4500 between 10 and 1. This means that on the clearest night we cannot see many more than 2000 stars. Most people would estimate the number to be far higher.

The planets do not shine with their own light, but reflect the light of the Sun. Their brightness in the sky depends both on how much of the surface is illuminated and on how far away they are. Venus at its brightest is equal to 13,000 units and if it is visible, it is the brightest object in the sky. The brightest of the other planets is given in this diagram.

Incidentally, the brightness of a full Moon is 26,000,000 units and of the full Sun 16,000,000,000,000 units.

STELLAR MAGNITUDES

It may seem remarkable that we are able to see very faint stars of brightness one unit and yet not be blinded by the brightness of the Sun, or indeed by the Moon or Venus. However, our eyes do not respond to the number of units but more to the logarithm of the number of units. The traditional scale for measuring brightness uses the number 6 for the faintest visible star and works downwards. A star of magnitude 5 is about twice as bright as one of magnitude 6. A star of magnitude 4 is about twice as bright as magnitude 5 and so on. Unfortunately, by working backwards like this there are problems because some stars are brighter than magnitude 0. The solution is to continue the scale into negative numbers. There are only four stars which have negative magnitudes.

Sirius -1.45, Canopus -0.73, Alpha Centauri -0.10, Arcturus -0.06.

13

SOME IMPORTANT FEATURES OF THE NIGHT SKY

Certain constellations are more easily recognisable than others and will serve as pointers or markers to the less known ones. On the Star-Globe they are joined by red lines.

Polaris

URSA MAJOR - *Merak Dubhe*
THE GREAT BEAR

This constellation is also known as 'The Big Dipper' or 'The Plough' and in Europe and North America it is always visible. Two of the stars Dubhe and Merak point to the Pole Star and therefore are very useful in finding north.

CASSIOPEIA

This constellation forms a clear W shape on the other side of the Pole Star from The Plough and is clearly within the Milky Way. Bisect the angles of the W to point roughly to the Pole Star.

Andromeda +
Spiral

SQUARE OF PEGASUS

While not exactly a square, it is a clearly marked quadrilateral and it serves as a useful reference point in this part of the sky. Not far away is the Andromeda spiral which can just be seen with the naked eye on a very clear night. It looks like a misty patch, not a star.

Sirius

ORION AND SIRIUS

Orion is perhaps the finest constellation in the sky and being on the celestial equator, it is visible from all parts of the Earth. The brightest star Sirius is not far away from Orion but it is not part of the constellation. It belongs to Canis Major.

THE SOUTHERN CROSS

Although very small, the constellation Crux is most impressively bright. It can only be seen from south of 26°N and so was not seen by Europeans until they began their voyages of exploration and emigration.

The Pleiades

Aldebaran

THE PLEIADES

When this splendid group of stars in the constellation of Taurus is above the horizon, you will not be able to miss them. Only six can be seen with the naked eye, but through binoculars or a telescope there are many more.

6

15

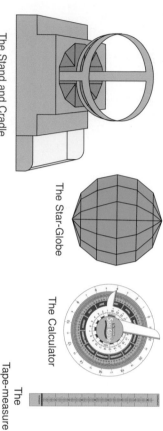

The Stand and Cradle

The Star-Globe

The Calculator

The Tape-measure

The Star-Globe will fit into the cradle in any position and the half of the celestial sphere which then appears above the horizon is a real sky which could be seen from somewhere on Earth at some time. However, the directions on the horizon ring are only correct when the axis of the Star-Globe lies in a north-south direction. Let us deal with the northern and southern hemispheres separately.

THE NORTHERN HEMISPHERE

The most important point to remember is that the north celestial pole, which is very close to Polaris, the Pole Star, is always due north of you and must always be directly above the northern horizon. The elevation of the north celestial pole is always equal to the latitude of observation, and that fact allows us to set the axis correctly.

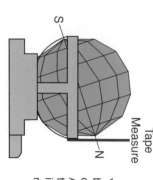

Tape Measure

S

N

You can set the celestial axis to its correct angle by placing the south celestial pole against the chosen latitude on the south side of the cradle. Alternatively, and more accurately, you can use the tape-measure to check that the north celestial pole is indeed at the correct angle of latitude above the northern horizon.

This procedure fixes the axis of the Star-Globe in the correct north-south direction and at the correct angle for your chosen latitude. Keeping the axis fixed we are able to rotate the Star-Globe through 360°, just as the real sky appears to turn through 360° because of the rotation of the Earth.

FINDING JUPITER

Jupiter, the greatest of the planets, has an orbit far larger than the Earth. It lies always on the ecliptic, and takes almost exactly 12 years to complete its circuit of the celestial sphere. It moves through approximately 2 hours of R.A. during each year, and it is useful to mark its position on the Star-Globe by using a circle of sticky paper. It need only be moved every three or four months, because Jupiter is so bright that you will be quite sure that you have found it. Jupiter has four moons which can be seen easily through binoculars, and which change their position from night to night.

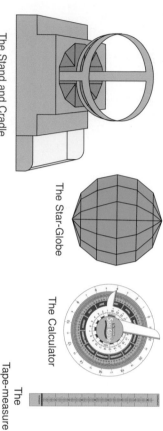

JUPITER

FINDING SATURN

Saturn takes almost 30 years to complete its circuit around the ecliptic, and moves less than one hour of R.A. each year. The chart gives its position during half a circuit. Saturn remains fixed in direction relative to the plane of the ecliptic and so its brightness varies according to the angle from which we observe its famous rings. It is brightest at intervals of 14 years and has a maximum brightness in the years 2001, 2015, 2029 etc. Between these dates the rings are seen more edge on from Earth and the planet appears rather less bright. It has a minimum brightness in the years 2008, 2022, 2036 etc.

SATURN

FINDING MARS

The orbit of Mars lies outside the orbit of the Earth and could therefore theoretically be represented by a chart like the ones for Jupiter and Saturn. However, although it does always lie close to the ecliptic, it does not appear to advance along it at a steady pace. Because the orbits of Earth and Mars are close together Mars appears from Earth to advance along the ecliptic for 710 days and then to retrace its steps for a further 70 days. Only at intervals of 780 days does it occupy the same position in the sky. Newspapers and magazines often publish a monthly star chart with the planets marked on it and that is probably the best way to know where to look. Occasionally Mars is brighter than Jupiter, but mostly it is much fainter. It does however have a reddish colour.

FINDING THE MOON

If the Moon is visible at all, then there is no problem in finding it! Indeed it can make seeing the stars rather difficult. The moon does not stray far from the ecliptic, but its motion is too complicated to be able to forecast its position with only simple charts.

USING THE CALCULATOR

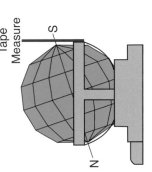

Turn the central disc to set the date. Then turn the arm to set the time on the central disc. Remember that it works on natural time, and if 'Summer Time' or 'Daylight Saving Time' is in operation, you will need to deduct one hour from clock or watch time. Now read off the R.A. number from the outer edge of the disc. This number tells you where to turn the Star-Globe. Turn it so that the meridian with that number leads between the north celestial pole and the northern horizon. Make sure that the north celestial pole is still at the correct angle above the horizon.

The sky is now set up for the required latitude, date and time. The horizon ring on the cradle then shows what you will be able to see in every direction. The stars which are directly overhead are at the top of the Star-Globe. If you want to know how many degrees above the horizon a particular star is, then use the tape-measure. Start your observations of the night sky by picking out some of the well-known constellations and bright stars.

overhead →

THE SOUTHERN HEMISPHERE

Tape Measure

S

N

The method for latitudes in the southern hemisphere is exactly the same, except that it is the southern celestial pole which is above the southern horizon at an angle equal to the latitude. The calculator is used in the same way, but you have to set the meridian with the correct R.A. number so that it leads between the south celestial pole and the southern horizon.

Questions: How should the Star-Globe be set up on the equator? How should it be set up at the north and south poles?

8

FINDING THE PLANETS

Since the brightest objects in the night sky after the Sun and Moon are the planets Venus, Jupiter, Saturn and Mars, we need to find a method of identifying them. The planets move too quickly across the celestial sphere to be printed on the Star-Globe itself. However, they do lie close to the ecliptic, and we can make some small sticky labels to mark their positions as we did for the Sun. As long as we are looking roughly in the right direction we shall certainly see them. And once we have identified a bright planet, we can often use it to identify other nearby stars. Planets do not twinkle as much as stars do, and that is a good way to confirm that you have actually found one. The planets Uranus, Neptune and Pluto are too faint to see without optical help, and Mercury is difficult to observe as it is usually lost in the glare of the Sun.

FINDING VENUS

VENUS

Venus is closer to the Sun than the Earth and so its position in the sky is never more than 3 hours of R.A. from the position of the Sun. We can use the calculator disc to find the R.A. of the Sun on any date, and then add or subtract the number given in the table below.

Example: Find the position of Venus on October 14th 2013.

On October 14th the R.A. of the Sun is 14. From the table below, Venus is at +3. The R.A. of Venus is roughly at 14 + 3 = 17, and it is on the ecliptic. It is close to Antares and the Galactic Centre. A year earlier on October 14th 2012 it is at 14 - 3 = 11, near Regulus.

YEARS	J	F	M	A	M	J	J	A	S	O	N	D	
2000, 2008	-2	-2	-1	0	0	0	+1	+1	+2	+2	+3	+3	These values are approximate, but Venus is so bright that you will not be able to miss it. Add the appropriate number to the R.A. of the Sun. Every eight years the position of Venus repeats itself.
2001, 2009	+3	+3	+1	0	-3	-3	-3	-2	-2	-1	-1	0	
2002, 2010	0	-1	+1	+2	+2	+2	+3	+3	+2	0	-1	-3	
2003, 2011	-3	-3	-3	-2	-2	-1	-1	0	0	+1	+2	+2	
2004, 2012	+2	+3	+3	+3	+2	0	0	-2	-3	-3	-2	-2	
2005, 2013	-1	0	0	0	+1	+1	+2	+2	+3	+3	+3	+2	
2006, 2014	0	-2	-3	-3	-3	-2	-2	-1	-1	0	0	+1	
2007, 2015	+1	+2	+2	+3	+3	+3	+2	0	0	-2	-3	-3	

When the figure in the table is +, then Venus can be seen in the evening after the Sun has set. When it is -, it can be seen before dawn. When the number is 0, Venus is lost in the glare of the Sun.

11

THE SUN AND THE ECLIPTIC

As the Earth completes its orbit around the course of a year, the Sun appears to trace out a path around the celestial sphere. This apparent path is called the 'ECLIPTIC' and it is marked in red on the Star-Globe. The Sun reaches approximately the same point on the ecliptic on the same date each year.

This diagram gives the R.A. of the Sun on each day of the year. You will notice that it is the same as the base disc of the calculator. The easiest way to find the position of the Sun on any date is to use the calculator. Because the ecliptic is inclined to the equator, and because the Earth's orbit is not quite circular, the R.A. of the Sun does not change quite as regularly as this chart suggests but the difference is small and it will serve our purposes well. We can now use the Star-Globe to find out interesting facts about the daytime as well as about the night sky.

Investigation: Find the position of the Sun on September 10th.

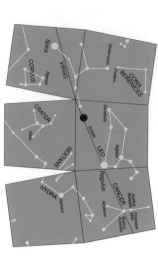

Using the calculator disc, we can see that on September 10th the R.A. of the Sun is between 11 and 12. It must lie on the ecliptic and must therefore be at the position shown on this chart. It lies midway between the two bright stars Spica and Regulus.

If the Sun is above the horizon, then neither star can be seen. However, there is a time just before dawn and just after sunset when one of them can be seen just above the horizon.

Now we know where the Sun is, we can attach a small sticky circle to the Star-Globe in the correct position. Do choose a type of self-adhesive label to cut from which will not damage the surface of the Star-Globe. You will wish to keep the Sun moving around the ecliptic as the year progresses.

THE SUN ON THE STAR-GLOBE INVESTIGATION

Set up the Star-Globe for 11.30am on September 10th at latitude 52°N.

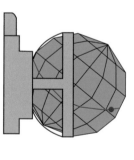

Follow the usual method to set up the Star-Globe. Remember that Summer Time is in operation and it is therefore necessary to set the dial to 10.30am.

You will find that it is the meridian 22 which leads from the north celestial pole to the northern horizon. The angle is 52°.

When you look at the sky you will see that the Sun is above the horizon, and therefore that it is daytime! You can also see that the Sun is slightly east of south on a bearing of about 150°, and that by using the tape measure the elevation is about 40°.

Notice that 90 minutes later at noon, the Star-Globe is due South, as it should be! The elevation of the Sun is then about 43°, which is the maximum for that day.

SUNRISE AND SUNSET INVESTIGATION

Find the bearing and time of sunset on September 10th at latitude 52°N.

When the Sun is exactly on the horizon on the western side of the sky, then it must be sunset. We must rotate the Star-Globe, keeping the axis at 52°, until this happens. Then the sky is set for sunset. You will see that the Sun is then a little to the north of west, (bearing between 275° and 280°). The Sun therefore sets on that date at that latitude at about 278°. Additionally, we can use the calculator to see what time sunset will be. The meridian which leads between the north celestial pole and the northern horizon now has R.A. = 6. If we set the calculator to September 10th and the 'answer' to 6 then the time is 18.30. The calculator does not take account of Summer Time, which would be in operation at that date. Hence the Sun will set at about 19.30.

Just after sunset on September 10th at latitude 52°N, the star Spica could just be seen low over the western horizon.

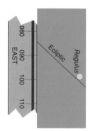

Just before sunrise on September 10th at latitude 52°N, the star Regulus could just be seen low over the eastern horizon.

You can now find sunrise and sunset on any date at any attitude, using your Star-Globe. Try also to decide which stars are visible just before dawn and just after sunset. Try it for today at your own latitude!

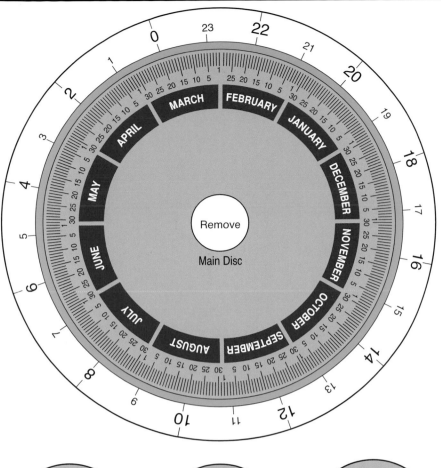

Main Disc

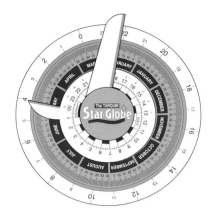

1. Cut out all the pieces and the five central circles.

2. Score along the dotted line on the pivot. Cut the 'teeth' and fold towards you.

3. Score and fold the frame for the time disc. Spread glue inside the fold and press firmly. When dry, cut out the time disc looking at the side marked 'cut this side'.

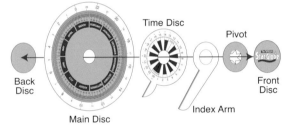

Back Disc

Main Disc

Time Disc

Pivot

Front Disc

Index Arm

4. Score, fold and glue the index arm as indicated. When dry, cut around the marked circle.

5. Assemble the central four pieces in the order shown in the diagram. The pivot teeth pass through the centre holes and join the pieces together. Glue the pivot teeth to the back of the main disc using only flaps D. The time disc and the index arm must turn freely and independently.

6. Use the letters E and F to position the front disc and the back disc.

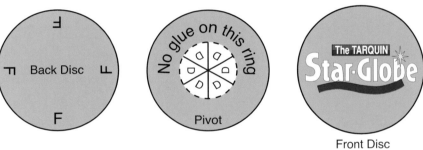

Back Disc

No glue on this ring

Pivot

The TARQUIN
Star·Globe

Front Disc

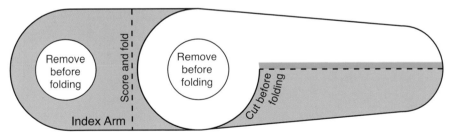

Remove before folding

Score and fold

Remove before folding

Cut before folding

Index Arm

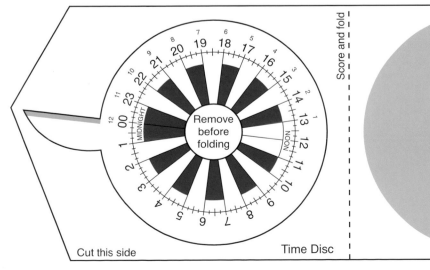

Remove before folding

Score and fold

Remove before folding

Cut this side

Time Disc

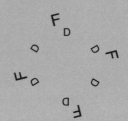

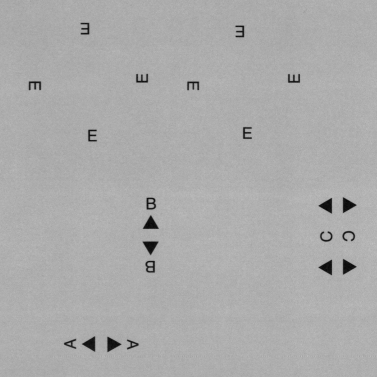

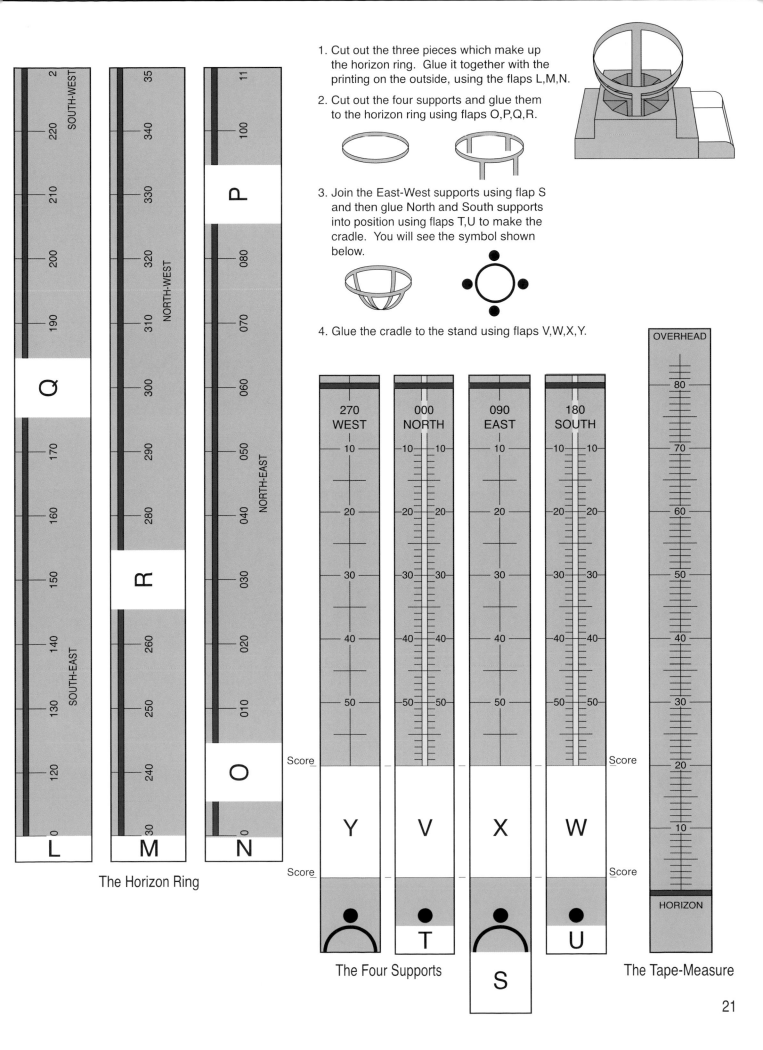

1. Cut out the three pieces which make up the horizon ring. Glue it together with the printing on the outside, using the flaps L,M,N.

2. Cut out the four supports and glue them to the horizon ring using flaps O,P,Q,R.

3. Join the East-West supports using flap S and then glue North and South supports into position using flaps T,U to make the cradle. You will see the symbol shown below.

4. Glue the cradle to the stand using flaps V,W,X,Y.

The Horizon Ring

The Four Supports

The Tape-Measure

L

M

Q   P   O   R

S

14

14

15

L

K

15

15

L

K

L

K

26

28A

26

28B

27A

28C

27B

28D

27C

29

28E

27D

27E

29

G

H

H

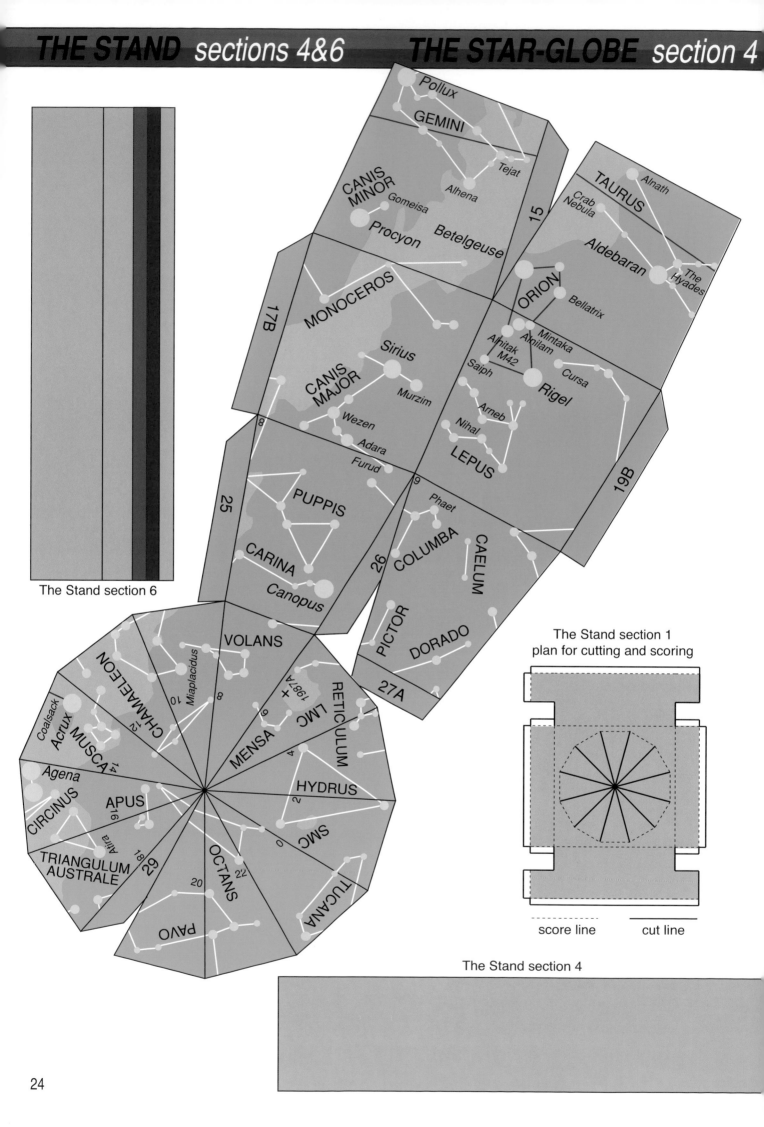

The Stand section 6

GEMINI

Pollux

CANIS MINOR

Gomeisa

Procyon

Betelgeuse

15

TAURUS

Alnath

Crab Nebula

Aldebaran

The Hyades

Tejat

Alhena

17B

MONOCEROS

ORION

Bellatrix

Mintaka

Anilam

Alnitak M42

Sirius

Saiph

Cursa

CANIS MAJOR

Murzim

Rigel

8

Wezen

Arneb

Adara

Nihal

19B

Furud

LEPUS

25

9

Phaet

PUPPIS

COLUMBA

CAELUM

26

CARINA

Canopus

PICTOR

DORADO

27A

VOLANS

Miaplacidus

CHAMAELEON

10

8

RETICULUM

1987A

LMC

Coalsack

Acrux

MUSCA

12

MENSA

6

Agena

14

4

HYDRUS

CIRCINUS

APUS

16

2

SMC

Alfira

18

OCTANS

TRIANGULUM AUSTRALE

29

22

TUCANA

20

PAVO

The Stand section 1
plan for cutting and scoring

- - - - - score line   ——— cut line

The Stand section 4

D

A   A

A   A

D

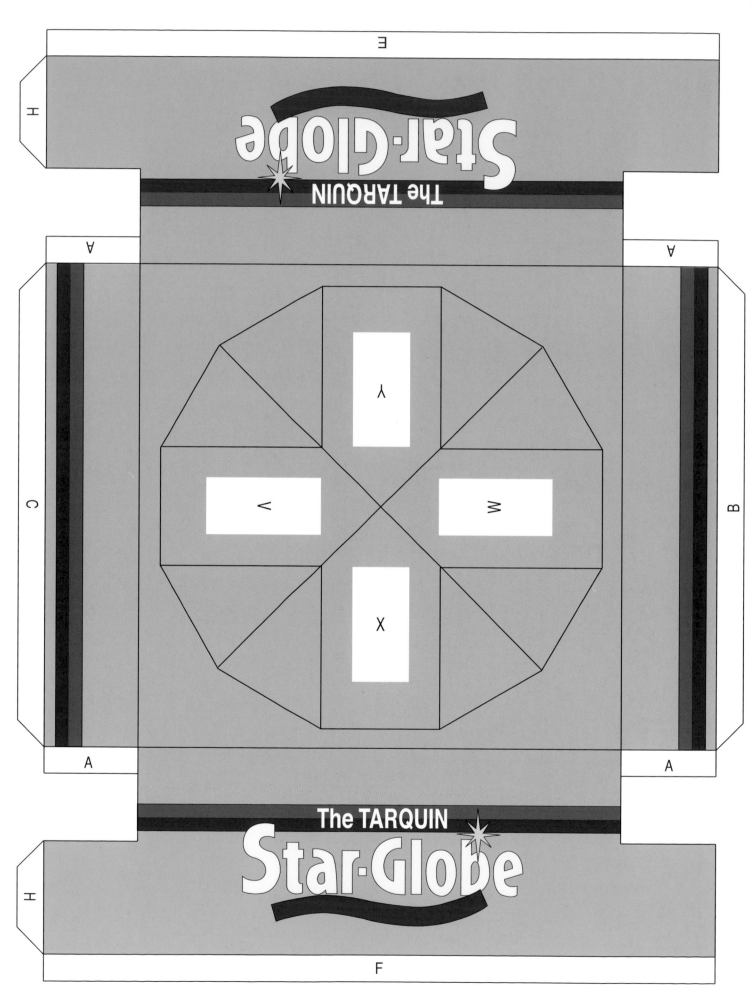

Ǝ

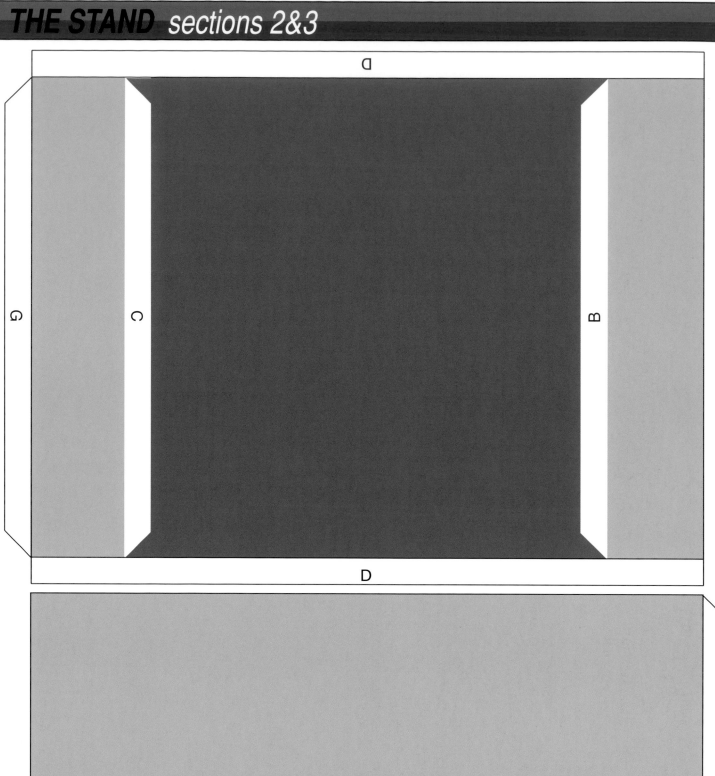

A

G

C

B

D

D

H